NURSERY RHYMES

JACK AND JILL

Jack and Jill went up the hill
To fetch a pail of water;
But they were whisked up in the sky,
To live on the moon ever after.

LITTLE JACK HORNER

Little Jack Horner
Sat in a corner,
Eating his Christmas pie;
He put in his thumb,
And pulled out a plum,
And said,
" What a good boy am I !"

LITTLE POLLY FLINDERS

Little Polly Flinders
Sat among the cinders,
Warming her pretty little toes !
Her mother came and caught her,
And whipped her little daughter
For spoiling her nice new clothes.

A BUNCH OF BLUE RIBBONS

Oh dear, what can the matter be?
Oh dear, what can the matter be?
Oh dear, what can the matter be?
Johnny's so long at the fair.

He promised he'd buy me a
    bunch of blue ribbons,
He promised he'd buy me a
    bunch of blue ribbons,
He promised he'd buy me a
    bunch of blue ribbons,
To tie up my bonny brown hair.

WEE WILLIE WINKIE

Wee Willie Winkie runs through
the town,
Upstairs and downstairs, in his
nightgown;
Rapping at the window, crying
through the lock,
"Are the children in their beds?
For now it's eight o'clock."

TOM, TOM, THE PIPER'S SON

Tom, Tom, the piper's son,
Stole a pig, and away he ran,
The pig was eat, and Tom was beat,
And Tom went crying down the street.

ROCK-A-BYE, BABY

Rock-a-bye, baby, on the tree top!
When the wind blows,
    the cradle will rock;
When the bough breaks,
    the cradle will fall;
Down will come baby, cradle and all.

HE THAT WOULD THRIVE

He that would thrive must rise at five,
He that hath thriven may lie till seven,
And he that by the plough would thrive,
Himself must hold or drive.

DAVY, DAVY DUMPLING

Davy, Davy Dumpling,
Put him in the pot,
Sugar him and butter him,
And eat him while he's hot.

POLLY, PUT THE KETTLE ON

Polly, put the kettle on,
Polly, put the kettle on,
Polly, put the kettle on,
And let's drink tea.

Sukey, take it off again,
Sukey, take it off again,
Sukey, take it off again,
They're all gone away.

A LITTLE GIRL WITH A CURL

There was a little girl
    and she had a little curl,
Right in the middle of her forehead.
When she was good,
    she was very, very good,
But when she was bad,
    she was horrid.

DING, DONG, BELL

Ding, dong, bell,
Pussy's in the well!
Who put her in?
Little Johnny Green.
Who pulled her out?
Little Johnny Stout.
What a naughty boy was that
To try to drown poor Pussy-cat,
Who never did him any harm,
But killed the mice
    in his father's barn.

BAA, BAA, BLACK SHEEP

Baa, baa, black sheep, have you any wool?
Yes, sir! yes, sir!—three bags full;
One for my master, one for my dame,
And one for the little boy who lives down the lane.

THE QUEEN OF HEARTS

The Queen of Hearts,
She made some tarts,
All on a summer's day.
The Knave of Hearts,
He stole the tarts,
And took them clean away.

The King of Hearts
Called for the tarts,
And beat the Knave full sore.
The Knave of Hearts
Brought back the tarts,
And vowed he'd steal no more.

JANUARY

January brings the snow,
Makes our feet and fingers glow.

FEBRUARY

February brings the rain,
Thaws the frozen lake again.

MARCH

March brings breezes loud and shrill,
Stirs the dancing daffodil.

APRIL

April brings the primrose sweet,
Scatters daisies at our feet.

MAY

May brings flocks of pretty lambs,
Skipping by their fleecy dams.

JUNE

June brings tulips, lilies, roses,
Fills the children's hands with posies.

JULY

Hot July brings cooling showers.
Apricots and pretty flowers.

AUGUST

August brings the sheaves of corn,
Then the harvest home is borne.

SEPTEMBER

Warm September brings the fruit,
Sportsmen then begin to shoot.

OCTOBER

Fresh October brings the pheasant,
Then to gather nuts is pleasant.

NOVEMBER

Dull November brings the blast,
Then the leaves are whirling fast.

DECEMBER

Chill December brings the sleet,
Blazing fire and Christmas treat.

MISTRESS MARY, QUITE CONTRARY

Mistress Mary, quite contrary,
How does your garden grow?
With silver bells and cockle shells
And pretty maids all in a row.

LITTLE MISS MUFFET

Little Miss Muffet sat on a tuffet,
Eating her curds and whey;
Then came a big spider,
Who sat down beside her,
And frightened Miss Muffet away!

ALAS! ALAS!
FOR MISS MACKAY!

Alas! Alas! for Miss Mackay!
Her knives and forks have run away;
And where the cups and spoon are going,
She's sure there is no way of knowing.

THERE WAS AN OLD WOMAN

There was an old woman who lived in a shoe,
She had so many children, she didn't know what to do.
She gave them some broth, without any bread,
Then whipped them all soundly and sent them to bed.

PRAYER

There are four corners on my bed.
There are four angels at its head.
Matthew, Mark, Luke and John,
Bless the bed that I lie on.

TWINKLE, TWINKLE

Twinkle, twinkle, little star,
How I wonder what you are!
Up above the world so high,
Like a diamond in the sky.

CURLY-LOCKS

Curly-locks! Curly-locks!
  Wilt thou be mine?
Thou shalt not wash dishes,
  nor yet feed swine;
But sit on a cushion,
  and sew a fine seam
And feed upon strawberries,
  sugar, and cream!

I LOVE LITTLE PUSSY

I love little pussy, her coat is so warm,
And if I don't hurt her, she'll do me no harm;
I'll not pull her tail nor drive her away,
But pussy and I very gently will play.

SIMPLE SIMON

Simple Simon met a pieman
  Going to the fair;
Said Simple Simon to the pieman,
  " Let me taste your ware."

Said the pieman to Simple Simon,
  " Show me first your penny."
Said Simple Simon to the pieman,
  " Indeed, I haven't any."

OLD MOTHER HUBBARD

Old Mother Hubbard
Went to the cupboard,
To fetch her poor dog a bone;
But when she got there
The cupboard was bare
And so the poor dog had none.

She took a clean dish
To get him some tripe;
But when she came back
He was smoking a pipe.

She went to the fruiterer's
To buy him some fruit;
But when she came back
He was playing the flute.

She went to the tailor's
To buy him a coat;
But when she came back
He was riding a goat.

She went to the hatter's
To buy him a hat;
But when she came back
He was feeding the cat.

She went to the hosier's
To buy him some hose,
But when she came back
He was dressed in his clothes.

The dame made a curtsey,
The dog made a bow;
The dame said, "Your servant,"
The dog said, "Bow-wow."

CUSHY COW

Cushy cow, cushy cow, give me your milk,
And I will give you a gown of silk;
A gown of silk and a silver tee,
If you will give your milk to me.

HEY DIDDLE DIDDLE

Hey diddle diddle,
The cat and the fiddle,
The cow jumped over the moon;
The little dog laughed
To see such sport,
And the dish ran away with the spoon.

THE MILLER

The miller he grinds his corn, his corn,
Little Boy Blue comes blowing his horn,
With a hop, a skip and a jump.
The carter he whistles aside his team.
And Dolly makes lots of clotted cream,
With a hop, a skip and a jump.

BELL HORSES

Bell horses, bell horses,
What time of day?
One o'clock, two o'clock,
Time to away.

IF I HAD A DONKEY

If I had a donkey
That would not go,
Would I whip him?
No, no, no!
I'd put him in a barn
And give him some corn,
The best little donkey
That ever was born.

I HAD A LITTLE HOBBY HORSE

I had a little hobby horse
And it was dapplc grey,
Its head was made of pea-straw,
Its tail was made of hay.

I sold him to an old woman
For a copper groat,
And I'll not sing my song again
Without a new coat

THREE YOUNG RATS

Three young rats
With black felt hats,
Three young ducks
With white straw flats,
Three young dogs
With curly tails,
Three young cats
With demi-veils,
Went out to walk
With two young pigs
In satin vests
And sorrel wigs.
But suddenly
It chanced to rain
And so they
All went home again.

THREE LITTLE KITTENS

Three little kittens they lost their mittens,
And they began to cry,
"Oh, mother dear, see here, see here,
That we have lost our mittens."
"What! Lost your mittens, you naughty kittens!
Then you shall have no pie.
Meeow, meeow, meeow,
No, you shall have no pie."

The three little kittens they found their mittens,
And they began to cry,
"Oh, mother dear, see here, see here,
For we have found our mittens."
"Put on your mittens, you silly kittens,
And you shall have some pie.
Purrr, purrr, purrr,
Yes, you shall have some pie."

I HAD A LITTLE HEN

I had a little hen,
The prettiest ever seen;
She washed up the dishes,
And kept the house clean.
She went to the mill
To fetch me some flour,
And always got home
In less than half an hour.
She baked me my bread,
She brewed me my ale,
She sat by the fire
And told me a fine tale.

GOOSEY GOOSEY GANDER

Goosey, goosey gander,
Whither shall I wander?
Upstairs and downstairs
And in my lady's chamber.
There I met an old man
Who would not say his prayers.
I took him by the left leg
And threw him down the stairs.

LITTLE ROBIN REDBREAST

Little Robin Redbreast
Came to visit me;
This is what he whistled
"Thank you for my tea."

JENNY WREN FELL SICK

Jenny Wren fell sick
Once upon a time,
In came Robin Redbreast
And brought her sops and wine.

"Eat well of the sop, Jenny,
Drink well of the wine."
"Thank you, Robin, kindly
You shall be mine."

Jenny Wren got well,
And stood upon her feet;
And told Robin plainly,
She loved him not a bit.

Robin he got angry,
And hopped upon a twig,
Saying, "Out upon you, fie upon you!
Bold faced jig!"

PIT PAT WELL A DAY

Pit, pat, well-a-day,
Little Robin flew away;
Where can little Robin be?
Gone into a cherry tree.

A CAT CAME FIDDLING
OUT OF A BARN

A cat came fiddling out of a barn,
With a pair of bagpipes under her arm;
She could sing nothing but "Fiddle-de-dee,
The mouse has married the bumble-bee."
Pipe, cat; dance, mouse;
We'll have a wedding at our good house.

DIDDLETY DIDDLETY DUMPTY

Diddlety, diddlety, dumpty,
The cat ran up the plum tree;
Half a crown
To fetch her down,
Diddlety, diddlety, dumpty.

PUSSY CAT SITS BY THE FIRE

Pussy cat sits by the fire,
So pretty and so fair.
In walks a little dog,
"Ah, Pussy, are you there?
How do you do, Mistress Pussy?
Mistress Pussy, how do you do?"
"I thank you kindly, little dog,
I'm very well and you?"

PUSSY CAT MOLE

Pussy Cat Mole jumped over a coal,
And in her best petticoat burned a great hole.
Poor pussy's weeping, she'll have no more milk
Until her best petticoat is mended with silk.

THERE WAS A CROOKED MAN

There was a crooked man
Who walked a crooked mile,
He found a crooked sixpence
Beside a crooked stile;
He bought a crooked cat,
Which caught a crooked mouse,
And they all lived together
In a little crooked house.

HICKORY DICKORY DOCK

Hickory, dickory, dock,
The mouse ran up the clock.
The clock struck one,
The mouse ran down,
Hickory, dickory, dock.

LITTLE POLL PARROTT

Little Poll Parrot
Sat in his garret
Eating toast and tea;
A little brown mouse,
Jumped into the house,
And stole it all away.

THIS LITTLE PIG
WENT TO MARKET

This little pig went to market,
This little pig stayed home,
This little pig had roast beef,
This little pig had none,
And this little pig cried "Wee-wee-wee,
I can't find my way home."

BARBER BARBER
SHAVE A PIG

Barber, barber, shave a pig,
How many hairs will make a wig?
Four and twenty, that's enough.
Give the barber a pinch of snuff.

A LONG-TAILED PIG

A long-tailed pig,
Or a short-tailed pig,
Or a pig without a tail.
A boar pig, or a sow pig,
Or a pig with a curly tail.
Take hold of its tail, and bite off its head,
For this is a pig made from sweet gingerbread.

TOM HE WAS A PIPER'S SON

Tom, he was a piper's son,
He learned to play when he was young,
But all the tune that he could play
Was 'Over the hills and far away'.

Tom with his pipe did play with such skill
That those who heard him could never keep still;
As soon as he played they began for to dance,
Even pigs on their hind legs would after him prance.

As Dolly was milking her cow one day,
Tom took up his pipe and began to play;
And Dolly and her cow danced 'The Cheshire Round',
Till the pail was broken and the milk ran on the ground.

Tom saw a cross fellow was beating an ass,
Heavy ladened with pots, pans, dishes and glass;
He took out his pipe and he played them a tune,
And the poor donkey's load was lightened very soon.

HARK

Hark, hark,
The dogs do bark,
The beggars are coming to town;
Some in rags,
And some in jags,
And one in a velvet gown.

HODDLEY PODDLEY

Hoddley, poddley, puddle and fogs,
Cats are to marry the poodle dogs;
Cats in blue jackets, and dogs in red hats,
What will become of the mice and rats?

TWO LITTLE DOGS

Two little dogs
Sat by the fire
Over a fender of coal-dust;
Said one little dog
To the other little dog,
"If *you* don't talk, then why, *I* must."

PUSSYCAT PUSSYCAT

Pussycat, pussycat,
With a white foot,
When is your wedding?
For I'll come to it.
There's ale to brew,
And your cake to bake,
So pussycat, pussycat,
Don't be too late!

OLD MOTHER SHUTTLE

Old Mother Shuttle
Lived in a coal-scuttle
Along with her dog and cat;
What they ate I can't tell,
But 'tis known very well
That not one of the party was fat.

THE LITTLE BLACK DOG

The little black dog ran round the house,
And set the bull a-roaring,
And drove the monkey in the boat,
Who set the oars a-rowing,
And scared the cock upon the rock,
Who cracked his throat with crowing.

TWEEDLEDUM
AND TWEEDLEDEE

Tweedledum and Tweedledee
Agreed to have a battle,
For Tweedledum said Tweedledee
Had spoiled his nice new rattle.
Just then flew by a large black crow,
As big as a tar-barrel,
Which frightened both the heroes so,
They quite forgot their quarrel.

A ROBIN
AND A ROBIN'S SON

A robin and a robin's son
Went to town to buy a plum bun;
But the shop sold only plain,
And so they both came home again.

CAKES
FOR SALE

MAGPIES

See those magpies flying high?
They tell your fortune in the sky.
One for sorrow,
Two for joy,
Three for a letter,
Four for a toy.
Five for silver,
Six for gold,
Seven for a secret
Never to be told.

A WISE OLD OWL

A wise old owl lived in an oak;
The more he saw, the less he spoke.
The less he spoke, the more he heard.
Why can't we all be like that wise old bird?

SILVER

GOLD

AS I WAS GOING

As I was going to sell my eggs,
I met a sheep upon two legs,
Upon two legs, with crooked toes,
He tripped up his heels and fell on his nose.

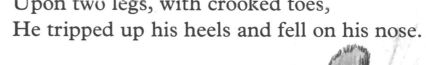

THE HART HE LOVES
THE HIGH WOOD

The hart he loves the high wood,
The hare she loves the hill;
The knight he loves his bright sword,
The lady loves her will.

THERE WAS
A RABBIT

There was a rabbit,
For want of stairs,
Went down a rope
To say his prayers.

ROCK-A-BYE, BABY

Rock-a-bye, baby,
Thy cradle is green,
Father's a nobleman,
Mother's a queen;
And Betty's a lady,
And wears a gold ring;
And Johnny's a drummer,
And drums for the king.

BYE, BABY BUNTING

Bye, baby bunting,
Daddy's gone a-hunting,
Gone to get a rabbit skin
To wrap our baby bunting in.

LIE STILL, MY BABY

Lie still, my baby, lie in thy cradle,
Mother has gone to buy a soup ladle;
When she comes back, she'll bring us some meat,
And daddy and baby shall have some to eat.

GO TO BED FIRST

Go to bed first,
A golden purse;
Go to bed second,
A golden pheasant;
Go to bed third,
A golden bird.

COME OUT TO PLAY

Girls and boys come out to play,
The moon doth shine as bright as day;
Leave your supper and leave your sleep,
And join your playfellows in the street.
Come with a whoop, come with a call,
Come with a good will or not at all.
Up the ladder and down the wall,
A half-penny roll will serve us all.
You find milk, and I'll find flour,
And we'll have a pudding in half an hour.

FRIDAY NIGHT'S DREAM

Friday night's dream
On the Saturday told
Is sure to come true,
Be it ever so old.

LITTLE FRED

When little Fred was called to bed,
He always acted right.
He kissed Mamma and then Pappa,
And went off with candle bright.

STAR LIGHT, STAR BRIGHT

Star light, star bright,
Hear the wish I make tonight;
And bright star, please do
Make my secret wish come true.

THE BRIGHT SILVER MOON

The bright silver moon is like a great can,
And in it, I'm told, is a nice little man;
Nurse saw him tonight,
With thumb in his eye,
And baby is listening to hear if he cry.

I SEE THE MOON

I see the moon,
And the moon sees me;
God bless the moon,
And God bless me.

TWINKLE, TWINKLE, LITTLE STAR

Twinkle, twinkle, little star,
How I wonder what you are!
Up above the world so high,
Like a diamond in the sky.

When the blazing sun is gone,
When he nothing shines upon,
Then you show your little light,
Twinkle, twinkle, all the night.

Then the traveller in the dark,
Thanks you for your little spark,
He could not see which way to go,
If you did not twinkle so.

In the dark blue sky you keep,
And often through my curtains peep,
For you never shut your eye,
Till the sun is in the sky.

THE MAN IN THE MOON
WAS CAUGHT IN A TRAP

The man in the Moon was caught in a trap
For stealing thorns from another man's gap.
If he had gone by, and let the thorns lie,
He'd never have become Man in the Moon so high.

DIDDLE, DIDDLE, DUMPLING

Diddle, diddle, dumpling, my son John,
Went to bed with his trousers on;
One shoe off, and one shoe on,
Diddle, diddle, dumpling, my son John.

ROBIN AND RICHARD

Robin and Richard
Were two pretty men,
They lay in bed
Till the clock struck ten;
Then up starts Robin
And looks at the sky,
"Oh, brother Richard,
The sun's very high.
You go before with
The bottle and bag,
And I will come after
On little Jack Nag."

THERE WAS AN OLD WOMAN

There was an old woman tossed high in a basket
Ninety times as high as the moon;
Where she was going I couldn't but ask it,
For in her hand she carried a broom.
"Old woman, old woman, old woman," quoth I,
"O whither, O whither, O whither so high?"
"To sweep the cobwebs from the night sky!"
"May I go with you?" "Yes, by and by."

LADYBIRD, LADYBIRD
Ladybird, Ladybird, fly away home;
The fieldmouse is gone to her nest,
The daisies have closed up their sleepy gold eyes,
And the birds and the bees are at rest.

ROCK-A-BYE
Rock-a-bye, baby, rock, rock, rock,
Baby shall have a new pink frock!
A new pink frock, and a ribbon to tie,
If you will sleep sweetly by and by.

EVENING RED
AND MORNING GREY

Evening red and morning grey:
Is the sign of a lovely day;
Evening grey and morning red:
The lamb and ewe go wet to bed.

EARLY TO BED

Early to bed,
And early to rise,
Is the way to be healthy,
And wealthy and wise.

ELSIE MARLEY

Elsie Marley's grown so fine
She won't get up to feed the swine,
But lies in bed till eight or nine,
Oh, lazy Elsie Marley!

THERE WAS A LITTLE MAID

There was a little maid
And she had a light guitar,
And when the moon was bright,
She sang tra, la, tra, la.

IF MY BOY SLEEPS QUIETLY

If my boy sleeps quietly,
He shall see a busy bee,
When it has made its honey fine,
Dancing in the bright sunshine.
If my boy will slumber,
Angels without number
Will draw near, so fair and bright,
For they only come at night.
If my boy will lie still in bed,
God, too, will be pleased and glad,
And will say, "I'll send to him
All night long the loveliest dream."

A GLASS OF MILK

A glass of milk,
A slice of bread,
And then we must
Go up to bed.

TO BED, TO BED

"To bed, to bed!"
Cried Sleepyhead.
"Tarry awhile,"
Said Slow.
"Put on the pan!"
Cried greedy Nan,
"We'll sup before we go."

SLEEP BABY, MY DOLLY

Sleep baby, my dolly, I pray you don't cry,
I'll give you milk when you awaken, by and by;
Or perhaps you like custard, or maybe a tart?
Then to either you're welcome, with all my heart.

QUIET THE NIGHT

Quiet the night,
Soft is the breeze;
Dim is the light
Of the faraway moon.
Sleep, children, sleep,
Be not alarmed,
Angels on guard,
Shall keep you unharmed.

WHAT SHALL YOU BUY?

What shall you buy?
A kite that will fly
Up to the moon,
All through the sky!
But if, when it gets there,
It should stay in the air,
Or the man in the moon
Should open the door,
And take it with his long, long paw—
We should sing another tune, oh!

THERE WAS AN OLD WOMAN
WHO LIVED BY THE SEA

There was an old woman who lived by the sea,
And she was as merry as merry could be.
She did nothing but carol from morning till night,
And sometimes she sang by candlelight.
She carolled in time and she carolled in tune,
But none cared to hear save the Man in the Moon.

THE CAT SAT ASLEEP BY THE FIRE

The cat sat asleep by the side of the fire,
When in walked a naughty young pig;
And woke him up rudely from out of his dreams
By playing a very loud jig!

CUSHY COW

Cushy cow, cushy cow, where do you lie?
In the green meadows under the sky.
Billy-horse, billy-horse, where do you lie?
Snug in a stable with nobody nigh.
Baby dear, baby love, where do you lie?
In my warm crib, with Mummy close by.

THERE CAME AN OLD WOMAN
FROM FRANCE

There came an old woman from France,
To teach all the children to dance;
But they all were so stiff, she sent them to bed in a sniff,
This sprightly old woman from France.

BEDFELLOWS

He that lies at the stock,
Shall have a golden rock;
He that lies at the wall,
Shall have a golden ball;
He that lies in the middle,
Shall have a golden fiddle.

TO MAKE YOUR CANDLES LAST

To make your candles last for ever,
You wives and maids give ear-o!
To put them out's the only way,
Says honest John Boldero.

GOLDEN SLUMBERS

Golden slumbers kiss your eyes,
Smiles awake you when you rise.
Sleep, pretty babies, do not cry,
And I will sing a lullaby;
Rock them, rock them, lullaby.
Care is heavy, therefore sleep you;
You are care, and care must keep you.
Sleep, pretty babies; do not cry,
And I will sing a lullaby;
Rock them, rock them, lullaby.

A GOOD CHILD

A good child, a good child,
As I suppose you be,
Before sleep say your prayers
At your mother's knee.

MATTHEW, MARK

Matthew, Mark, Luke and John,
Bless the bed that I lie on.
Four corners to my bed,
Four angels round my head;
One to sing, and one to pray,
And two to watch till break of day.

AND NOW, GOOD NIGHT

And now, good night; our play is done;
Farewell to each and everyone.

HOW MANY MILES
TO BABYLON?

How many miles to Babylon?
Three score miles and ten.
Can I get there by candlelight?
Yes, and back again.
If your horse be swift,
And your spurs be bright,
You may travel the world
By candlelight.

LONDON BRIDGE IS BROKEN DOWN

London Bridge is broken down,
Broken down, broken down,
London Bridge is broken down,
My fair lady.

I HAD A LITTLE HOBBY HORSE

I had a little hobby horse,
And it was well shod.
It took me to London
Niddetty nod.
And when we got to London,
I and my faithful beast,
We danced to the bagpipes,
And we had a great feast.

SEE-SAW, UP AND DOWN

See-saw, up and down,
Which is the way to London town?
One foot up and one foot down,
That is the way to London town.

MERCHANTS OF LONDON

Hey diddle dinkety, poppety pet,
The merchants of London they wear scarlet;
Silk in the collar and gold in the hem
So merrily march the merchant men.

NEAR ST. PAUL'S STEEPLE

Near St. Paul's steeple stands a tree
As full of apples as can be;
The little boys of London town
They run with hooks to pull them down:
And then they go from hedge to hedge
Until they come to London Bridge.

PUSSY CAT PUSSY CAT

Pussy cat, pussy cat, where have you been?
I've been to London to look at the queen.
Pussy cat, pussy cat, what did you there?
I frightened a little mouse under her chair.

AS I WAS GOING TO BANBUR

As I was going to Banbury
Upon a summer's day,
My dame had butter, eggs, and fruit,
And I had corn and hay;
Joe drove the ox, and Tom the swine,
Dick took the foal and mare,
I sold them all – then home to dine,
From famous Banbury fair.

RIDE A COCK HORSE
TO BANBURY CROSS

Ride a cock horse to Banbury Cross,
To see a fine lady upon a white horse;
Rings on her fingers and bells on her toes,
She shall have music wherever she goes.

RIDE A GREY MARE
TO BANBURY FAIR

Ride a grey mare,
To Banbury Fair,
To see what Tommy can buy;
A penny white loaf,
A penny white cake,
And a tuppenny apple pie.

THREE WISE MEN OF GOTHAM

Three wise men of Gotham,
Went to sea in a bowl,
And if the bowl had been stronger
My song had been longer.

THE MAN IN THE MOON

The man in the moon
Came down too soon,
And asked his way to Norwich;
He went to the south,
And burned his mouth
With eating cold pease porridge.

AS I WAS GOING TO ST. IVES

As I was going to St. Ives,
I met a man with seven wives,
Each wife had seven sacks,
Each sack had seven cats,
Each cat had seven kits:
Kits, cats, sacks, wives,
How many were going to St. Ives?

WHEN I WAS A LITTLE GIRL

When I was a little girl
About seven years old,
I had not a petticoat
To keep me from the cold.

So I went to Darlington,
That pretty little town,
And there I bought a petticoat,
A cloak and a gown.

LITTLE BOY, LITTLE BOY

Little Boy, little boy,
Where were you born?
Far away in Lancashire
Under a thorn,
Where they drink sour milk
From a ram's horn.

AS I WENT TO BONNER

As I went to Bonner
I met a pig
Wearing a wig,
Upon my word of honour.

DINGLE DINGLE DOOSEY

Dingle dingle doosey,
The cat's in the well,
The dog has gone to Bellingen
To buy the babe a bell.

AS I WAS GOING TO DERBY

As I was going to Derby,
Upon a market day,
I met the finest ram, sir,
That ever was fed on hay.

The wool upon his back, sir,
Reached up into the sky,
The eagles built their nests there,
For I heard the young ones cry.

This ram had four legs to walk upon,
This ram had four legs to stand,
And every leg he had, sir,
Stood on an acre of land.

Now, the man that fed the ram, sir,
He fed him twice a day,
And each time that he fed him, sir,
He ate a rick of hay.

OLD FARMER GILES

Old Farmer Giles
Walked seven miles
With his old dog Rover
Across the fields to Dover;
And old Farmer Giles,
When he came to the stiles,
Took a run and leaped clean over.

DOCTOR FOSTER WENT TO GLOUCESTER

Doctor Foster went to Gloucester
In a shower of rain;
He stepped in a puddle,
Right up to his middle,
And never went there again.

THERE WAS A JOLLY MILLER ONCE

There was a jolly miller once,
Lived by the River Dee;
He worked and sang from morn till night,
No lark more blithe than he.
And this the burden of his song
Forever used to be,
I care for nobody, no, not I!
If nobody cares for me.

OH, THE BRAVE OLD DUKE OF YORK

Oh, the brave old Duke of York,
He had ten thousand men;
He marched them up to the top of the hill,
And he marched them down again.
And when they were up, they were up,
And when they were down, they were down,
And when they were only half-way up,
They were neither up nor down.

THERE WAS AN OLD WOMAN
WHO LIVED IN DUNDEE

There was an old woman
Who lived in Dundee,
And in her back garden
There grew a plum tree.
She watered it daily
Till the plums grew ripe,
And sold them to callers
For three farthings a pint.

IN A COTTAGE IN FIFE

In a cottage in Fife
Lived a man and his wife,
Who, believe me, were comical folk;
For, to people's surprise,
They both saw with their eyes,
And their tongues moved whenever they spoke!
When quite fast asleep,
I've been told that to keep
Their eyes open they could not contrive;
They walked on their feet,
And 'twas thought what they eat
Helped, with drinking, to keep them alive!

A SCOTTISH PIPER HAD A COW

A Scottish piper had a cow,
And he had naught to give her.
So on his pipes he played a tune,
And bade the cow consider.

The cow considered very well,
And gave the piper a penny,
And bade him play another tune,
'Corn rigs are bonny'.

DOCTOR FOSTER WAS A GOOD MAN

Doctor Foster was a good man
Who taught his scholars how to dance
Out of Scotland, into France,
Out of France, into Spain,
And then he danced them home again.

THERE WAS AN OLD MAN OF THE BORDER

There was an old man of the Border,
Who lived in the utmost disorder,
He danced with his cat,
Made tea in his hat,
Which vexed all the folk of the Border.

BRYAN O'FLYNN WAS
AN IRISHMAN BORN

Bryan O'Flynn was an Irishman born,
His hair was curly, his beard was shorn;
He wore a cap made from rabbit skin,
A handsome man was Bryan O'Flynn.

BARNEY WAS
AN OLD MAN

Barney was an old man
Who lived in Middle Row,
He had five hens and he
Had a name for them, oh!
Bill and Ned and Battock,
Cut-her-foot and Pattock.
Chuck, my lady Pattock,
Go to your nest and lay.

THERE WERE THREE
JOVIAL WELSHMEN

There were three jovial Welshmen,
As I have heard men say,
And they went a-hunting
Upon St. David's Day.

All day they hunted
And nothing could they find
But a ship a-sailing,
A-sailing with the wind.

One said it was a ship,
The other he said nay,
The third said it was a house
With the chimney blown away.

And all night they hunted
And nothing could they find,
But the moon a-gliding,
A-gliding with the wind.

One said it was the moon,
The other he said nay,
The third said it was a cheese
And half of it cut away.

I HAD A LITTLE NUT TREE

I had a little nut tree,
Nothing would it bear
But a silver nutmeg
And a golden pear;
The king of Spain's daughter
Came to visit me,
And all for the sake
Of my little nut tree.

MY FATHER
WAS A FRENCHMAN

My father was a Frenchman,
A Frenchman, a Frenchman,
My father was a Frenchman,
And he bought me a fiddle.
I played it here,
I played it there,
I played it in the middle.

A TAILOR WHO
SAILED FROM QUEBEC

A tailor, who sailed from Quebec,
In a storm ventured once upon deck;
But the waves of the sea
Were as strong as can be,
And he tumbled in up to his neck.

YANKEE DOODLE
CAME TO TOWN

Yankee Doodle came to town,
Riding on a pony;
He stuck a feather in his cap
And called it macaroni.

TEN LITTLE INDIAN BOYS STANDING IN A LINE

Ten little Indian boys standing in a line,
One ran home quickly, and then there were nine.
Nine little Indians swinging on the gate,
One tumbled off, and then there were eight.
Eight little Indian boys, happiest under heaven,
One went fishing, and then there were seven.
Seven little Indian boys all full of tricks,
One of them went off to school, and then there were six.
Six little Indian boys, glad to be alive,
One went hunting and then there were five.

Five little Indians, playing round the door,
One went right outside, and then there were four.
Four little Indians went out to ski,
One stayed up the mountainside, and then there were three.
Three little Indians out in a canoe,
One of them went swimming, and then there were two.
Two little Indians sleeping in the sun,
One awoke and crept away, and then there was one.
One little Indian living all alone,
He got married, and then there were none.

THERE WAS AN OLD MAN OF TOBAGO

There was an old man of Tobago,
Who lived on rice, gruel, and sago;
Till, much to his bliss,
His physician said this,
"To a leg of mutton you may go."

AS A FAT MAN OF BOMBAY

As a little fat man of Bombay
Was smoking one very hot day,
A bird called a snipe
Flew away with his pipe,
Which vexed the fat man of Bombay.

THERE WAS A POOR MAN OF JAMAICA

There was a poor man of Jamaica,
Who opened a shop as a baker:
The nice biscuits he made
Procured him much trade
With all the little boys of Jamaica.

Mother Goose

OLD MOTHER GOOSE
Old Mother Goose,
When she wanted to wander,
Would ride through the air
On a very fine gander.

Mother Goose had a house,
'Twas built in a wood,
Where an owl at the door
For sentinel stood.

BOBBY SHAFTOE

Bobby Shaftoe's gone to sea,
With silver buckles at his knee:
He'll come back and marry me,
Pretty Bobby Shaftoe!

Bobby Shaftoe's fat and fair,
Combing down his yellow hair;
He's my love for evermore,
Pretty Bobby Shaftoe!

SEE-SAW, MARGERY DAW

See-saw, Margery Daw,
Johnny will have a new master;
He shall have but a penny a day
Because he can't work any faster.

I HAD A LITTLE PONY
I had a little pony,
His name was Dapple Grey;
I lent him to a lady,
To ride a mile away.
She whipped him, she lashed him,
She rode him through the mire;
I would not lend my pony now,
For all the lady's hire.

SING A SONG OF SIXPENCE
Sing a song of sixpence,
A pocket full of rye;
Four and twenty blackbirds
Baked in a pie.

When the pie was opened
The birds began to sing:
Was not that a dainty dish
To set before a king?

The king was in his counting-house,
Counting out his money;
The queen was in the parlour
Eating bread and honey.

The maid was in the garden,
Hanging out the clothes;
Down came a blackbird
And pecked off her nose.

COBBLER, COBBLER
Cobbler, cobbler, mend my shoe,
Get it done by half past two,
Stitch it up and stitch it down,
Then I'll give you half-a-crown.

EARLY TO BED
The cock crows in the morn
To tell us to rise,
And he that lies late
Will never be wise.

THREE BLIND MICE

Three blind mice, see how they run!
They all ran after the farmer's wife,
Who cut off their tails with a carving knife,
Did ever you see such a thing in your life,
As three blind mice?

ONE, TWO, THREE, FOUR, FIVE

One, two, three, four, five,
Once I caught a fish alive,
Six, seven, eight, nine, ten,
Then I let him go again.
Why did you let him go?
Because he bit my finger so.
Which finger did he bite?
This little finger on the right.

MARY HAD A LITTLE LAMB
Mary had a little lamb,
Its fleece was white as snow;
And everywhere that Mary went
The lamb was sure to go.

It followed her to school one day;
That was against the rule;
It made the childen laugh and play
To see a lamb at school.

OH WHERE, OH WHERE IS MY LITTLE DOG GONE?

Oh where, oh where is my little dog gone?
Oh where, oh where can he be?
With his ears cut short and his tail cut long,
Oh where, oh where is he?

IF ALL THE WORLD WERE APPLE PIE
If all the world were apple pie
And all the sea was ink,
And all the trees were bread and cheese,
What should we have to drink?

ORANGES AND LEMONS

Oranges and Lemons,
Say the bells of St. Clement's.
You owe me five farthings,
Say the bells of St. Martin's.
When will you pay me?
Say the bells of Old Bailey.
When I am rich,
Say the bells of Shoreditch.
When will that be?
Say the bells of Stepney.
I'm sure I don't know,
Says the great bell at Bow.
Here comes a candle to light
                   you to bed,
And here comes a chopper
        to chop off your head.
Chop, chop, chop, *chop*.

LITTLE BO-PEEP

Little Bo-peep has lost her sheep,
And doesn't know where to find them;
Leave them alone, and they'll come home,
Bringing their tails behind them.

HOT-CROSS BUNS

Hot-cross buns! Hot-cross buns!
One a penny, two a penny,
Hot-cross buns!
If you have no daughters,
Give them to your sons,
One a penny, two a penny,
Hot-cross buns!

MONDAY'S CHILD
Monday's child is fair of face,
Tuesday's child is full of grace,
Wednesday's child is full of woe,
Thursday's child has far to go,

Friday's child is loving and giving,
Saturday's child works hard for a living,
And the child that is born on the Sabbath day
Is bonny and blithe and good and gay.

HUMPTY DUMPTY

Humpty Dumpty sat on a wall,
Humpty Dumpty had a great fall;
All the King's horses and all the King's men
Couldn't put Humpty together again.

I SAW A SHIP A-SAILING

I saw a ship a-sailing,
A-sailing on the sea;
And, oh, it was all laden
With pretty things for thee!

There were comfits in the cabin,
And apples in the hold;
The sails were made of silk,
And the masts were made of gold.

The four and twenty sailors
That stood upon the decks,
Were four and twenty white mice,
With chains about their necks.

The captain was a duck,
With a jacket on his back;
And when the ship began to move,
The captain cried, "Quack! quack!"

WHEN JACKY'S A GOOD BOY

When Jacky's a good boy,
He shall have cakes and custard;
But when he does nothing but cry,
He shall have nothing but mustard.

A MAN IN THE WILDERNESS

A man in the wilderness said to me,
"How many strawberries grow in the sea?"
I answered him as I thought good,
"As many as red herrings grow in the wood."

TOMMY SNOOKS AND BESSY BROOKS

As Tommy Snooks and Bessy Brooks
Were walking out one Sunday,
Says Tommy Snooks to Bessy Brooks,
Tomorrow will be Monday.

THE QUEEN OF HEARTS

The Queen of Hearts
She made some tarts,
All on a summer's day.
The Knave of Hearts,
He stole the tarts,
And took them clean away.

The King of Hearts,
Called for the tarts,
And beat the Knave full sore.
The Knave of Hearts
Brought back the tarts,
And vowed he'd steal no more.

OLD KING COLE

Old King Cole was a merry old soul,
And a merry old soul was he;
He called for his pipe, he called for his bowl,
And he called for his fiddlers three.

Every fiddler, he had a fine fiddle,
And a very fine fiddle had he;
Oh, there's none so rare as can compare
With King Cole and his fiddlers three.

WHO COMES HERE?

Who comes here?
A grenadier.
What do you want?
A glass of beer.
Where is your money?
I've forgot.
Get you gone,
You can't have a drop.

CHERRY STONES

One, two, three, four,
Johnny's sitting on the floor,
Five, six, seven, eight,
Counting cherries on his plate.

MOLLY, MY SISTER AND I

Molly, my sister, and I fell out,
And what do you think it was all about?
She liked coffee, and I liked tea,
And that was the reason we didn't agree.

TO MARKET

I have been to market,
  my lady, my lady.
Then you've not been to the fair,
  says pussy, says pussy.
I bought me a rabbit,
  my lady, my lady.
Then you did not buy a hare,
  says pussy, says pussy.

JACK SPRAT

Jack Sprat could eat no fat,
His wife could eat no lean,
And so between them both,
They scraped the platter clean.

JACK AND JILL

Jack and Jill went up the hill
To fetch a pail of water;
Jack fell down and broke his crown,
And Jill came tumbling after.

Up Jack got, and home did trot,
As fast as he could caper.
His mother bandaged up his head
With vinegar and brown paper.

When Jill came in,
How she did grin
To see Jack's paper plaster,
Her mother whipped her very well
For laughing at Jack's disaster.

GEORGIE PORGIE

Georgie Porgie, pudding and pie,
Kissed the girls and made them cry;
When the boys came out to play,
Georgie Porgie ran away.

SKIPPER, SKIPPER

Skipper, skipper, whither bound?
To Providence and through the sound.
The storm is fierce; have you no fear?
The Guide of all will guide me there.

THE CUCKOO

The cuckoo is a fine bird,
He sings as he flies;
He brings us good tidings;
He never tells lies.
He drinks lots of water,
To make his voice clear,
And when he sings "Cuckoo!"
The springtime is here.

PANCAKE DAY

Great A, and little a,
This is pancake day;
Toss the ball high,
Throw the ball low,
Those that come after
May sing heigh-ho.

JENNY WREN LAST WEEK WAS WED

Jenny Wren last week was wed,
And built her nest in the woodpile shed;
Look in next week and you will see
Two little eggs, and maybe three.

THE MERCHANT MAN

The merchant man doth sail the seas,
And lie on the shipboard with little ease:
Always in doubt the rock is near,
How can he be merry and make good cheer?

But they do make merry and have great sport,
These sailors who're the bravest sort,
These men who sail the seven seas,
And work on the masts in twos and threes.

QUEEN OF MAY

Maid Marian is Queen of May,
All good children own her sway;
Her waist is white, her skirt is red,
A crown of gold is on her head.

RUB-A-DUB-DUB

Rub-a-dub-dub,
Three men in a tub;
And who do you think they be?
The butcher, the baker,
The candlestick maker;
Turn them out, knaves all three!

I HAD A LITTLE CASTLE

I had a little castle upon the seaside,
One half was water, the other was land;
I opened my castle door, and guess what I found?
I found a fair lady with a cup in her hand,
The cup was gold and filled with wine;
Drink, fair lady, and thou shalt be mine.

SUMMER BREEZE

Summer breeze, so softly blowing,
In my garden pinks are growing;
If you go and send the showers,
You may come and smell my flowers.

BUTTERFLY, BUTTERFLY

Butterfly, butterfly,
Whence do you come?
I know not, I ask not,
I never had a home.

Butterfly, butterfly,
Where do you go?
Where the sun shines, and
Where the buds grow.

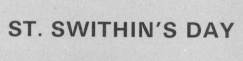

ST. SWITHIN'S DAY

St. Swithin's Day, if it doth rain,
For forty days it will remain;
St. Swithin's Day, if it be fair,
For forty days 'twill rain na mair.

ONE MISTY MOISTY MORNING

One misty moisty morning,
  when cloudy was the weather,
There I met an old man
  clothed all in leather;
Clothed all in leather,
  with his cap beneath his chin,
How do you do? And how do you do?
  And how do you do again!

HARVEST HOME

Harvest home, harvest home,
Ne'er a load's been overthrown.
Barns are full with grain and hay,
Food for all, for many a day.

ROAST CHESTNUTS

Chestnuts roasting by the fire,
If you love me,
Pop and fly,
If you dislike me,
Lie and die.

COME HITHER, SWEET ROBIN

Come hither, sweet robin, and be not afraid,
I would not hurt even a feather;
Come hither, sweet robin, and pick up some bread,
To feed you this very cold weather.

THE MUFFIN MAN

Do you know the Muffin Man,
The Muffin Man, the Muffin Man,
Do you know the Muffin Man,
That lives in Drury Lane?

Yes, we know the Muffin Man,
The Muffin Man, the Muffin Man,
Yes, we know the Muffin Man,
That lives in Drury Lane.

INCY WINCY SPIDER

Incy wincy spider climbed up the spout,
Down came the rain and washed the spider out.
Out came the sunshine,
Dried up all the rain,
Incy wincy spider climbed the spout again.

THE NORTH WIND

The north wind doth blow,
And we shall have snow,
And what will the robin do then, poor thing?
He'll sit in a barn
And keep himself warm,
And hide his head under his wing, poor thing.

The north wind doth blow,
And we shall have snow,
And what will the dormouse do then, poor thing?
Rolled up in a ball
In his nest snug and small,
He'll sleep until the weather is warm again, poor thing.

LITTLE TOMMY TITTLEMOUSE

Little Tommy Tittlemouse
Lived in a little house;
He caught fishes
In other men's ditches.

LITTLE DAME CRUMP

Little Dame Crump
With her little hair-broom
Was carefully sweeping
Her little bedroom.
"Hobs-bobs!" cried the Dame.
"A penny I spy,
To market I'll go
And a pig I will buy."

LITTLE GIRL, LITTLE GIRL

Little girl, little girl, where have you been?
Gathering roses to give to the Queen.
Little girl, little girl, what gave she you?
She gave me a diamond as big as my shoe.

LITTLE BETTY BLUE

Little Betty Blue
Lost her holiday shoe;
What can little Betty do?
Give her another,
To match the other,
And then she may walk in two.

LITTLE JACK-A-NORY

Little Jack-a-Nory
Told me a story,
How he tried
Cockhorse to ride,
Sword and scabbard by his side
Saddle,leaden spurs and switches,
His pocket tight
With pence all bright,
Marbles, tops, puzzles, props,
Now he's put in a jacket and breeches.

TOMMY TROT

Tommy Trot, a man of law,
Sold his bed and lay on straw;
Sold the straw and slept on grass,
To buy his wife a looking glass.

WHAT ARE LITTLE GIRLS MADE OF?

What are little girls made of?
What are little girls made of?
Sugar and spice, and all that's nice;
That's what little girls are made of.

LITTLE MAIDEN

Little maiden, better tarry,
Time enough next year to marry.
Hearts may change,
And so may fancy;
Wait a little longer, Nancy.

THE DAUGHTER OF THE FARRIER

The daughter of the farrier
Could find no one to marry her,
Because she said
She would not wed
A man who could not carry her.
The foolish girl was wrong enough,
And had to wait quite long enough;
For as she sat
She grew so fat
That nobody was strong enough.

THE COACHMAN

Up at Piccadilly, oh!
The coachman takes his stand,
And when he meets a pretty girl
He takes her by the hand;
Whip away forever, oh!
Drive away so clever, oh!
All the way to Bristol, oh!
He drives her four-in-hand.

FOUR-AND-TWENTY TAILORS

Four-and-twenty tailors went to kill a snail,
The best man amongst them durst not touch her tail;
She put out her horns like a little Kyloe cow,
Run, tailors, run, or she'll kill you all e'en now.

BESSIE BELL AND MARY GRAY

Bessie Bell and Mary Gray,
They were two bonny lasses,
They built their house upon the lea
And covered it with rushes.
Bessie kept the garden gate,
And Mary kept the pantry;
Bessie always had to wait,
While Mary lived in plenty.

ON SATURDAY NIGHT

On Saturday night
I'll take great care
To powder my locks
And curl my hair.
On Sunday morning
My love will come in,
And he will marry me
With a gold ring.